TUDOR AND EARLY STUART VOYAGES

D1526013

Tudor and Early Stuart Voyaging

BY BOIES PENROSE

FOLGER BOOKS

Published by
THE FOLGER SHAKESPEARE LIBRARY

FOR the first sixty-five years of the Tudor dynasty the story of English voyaging is sketchy and inconclusive. The impetus of a glowing beginning toward the end of the fifteenth century was not kept up, and for most of the reigns of Henry VII and Henry VIII English seafaring remains rather primitive, scanty alike in performance, organization, and records. Yet this era may be looked upon as the seedtime for the heroic age that was to follow, to bear fruit in the reign of Elizabeth.

There had, indeed, been for long a respectable maritime tradition in such ports as Bristol, where a trade in wines had for centuries existed with Bordeaux, as well as commerce with Seville in olive oil and Cordova leather and, more recently, with Iceland for fish in exchange for cloth. It was probably out of the last of these that the search for islands and lands to the westward began.

It is now thought that land (the "isle of Brasil," as they named it) was discovered by the English in the west, perhaps before Henry VII won the battle of Bosworth Field, though it may have been lost sight of again or, alternatively, kept secret as a valuable base for a fishery. There were voyages in search of it in 1480 and 1481, and the latter may have been successful—perhaps in finding Newfoundland and the Banks.

Into this setting came the Italian Giovanni Caboto, perhaps from Venice about 1486 or, possibly, it is now thought, from Spain in 1493 or 1494. He found that the leading families in Bristol, the Jays and Thornes and Eliots, were already engaged in western voyaging. It is still a matter for discussion whether Cabot joined with them as early as about 1490 or as late as 1494 or 1495, but there is little doubt that he added to their objectives the idea shared with Columbus of sailing westward to Asia across the Atlantic. He was able eventually to get their support for his daring venture and, after an unsuccessful voyage in 1495 or 1496, he set out in 1497 in the bark "Matthew" with a Bristol crew and, probably, his young son Sebastian.

Cabot's course is still in dispute, but it is likely that his landfall was in the vicinity of Cape Breton, after which he bore northeast along the southern and perhaps eastern shores of Newfoundland. Returning to Bristol after a mere three months, Cabot was convinced that he had found the mainland of Asia, though not the habitable part thereof, which by his reckoning must lie to the south. This conclusion brought him some support from Henry VII for a further voyage in 1498, the results of which remain most obscure. Cabot is thought to have been lost at sea, and nothing is certainly known of the extent of his discoveries. The Spaniards believed, as the celebrated La Cosa Map of 1500 (in the Museo Naval, Madrid) indicates, that he had sailed far enough south to have come within range of their newly found West Indian islands. Cabot had failed in his objective in that he did not discover Asia; his discovery of the North American mainland was incidental to his purpose. Nonetheless, he made known the existence of the magnificent Newfoundland fishery to which European fishermen of many nationalities were soon resorting.

In the years that followed (1501–1505) the Bristol merchants in association with some Portuguese from the Azores tried in a small way to trade with and explore the new lands. The Portuguese João Fernandes is associated with the discovery of Labrador, but otherwise the indications we have of their proceedings are slight and soon fade away. In 1508–1509 Sebastian Cabot, now grown to manhood, opened a new phase by attempting to sail round the new lands by a northwest passage, penetrating perhaps into Hudson Strait, but no farther. Three years after his return he left the English to become a cartographer in the Spanish service, becoming Pilot-Major of

MIL.AVR.

RIHARDVS GRENVILVS

Neptuni proles . qui magni Martis alumnus
GRENVILIVS patrias sanguine tinxit aguas

Plate 1. Sir Richard Grenville (1541–1591). Cornish aristocrat and cousin of Raleigh. Planted Roanoke colony, 1585.
Killed near Azores in heroic battle of the "Revenge" against
fifteen Spanish ships. From Henry Holland, *Herωologia*
(1620).

Spain in 1518, and with his departure the rather nebulous cycle of Bristol voyages of discovery comes to an end, even though her merchants appear to have sent out vessels regularly to the Newfoundland fishery.

Cabot could not have been sent to a better place than Seville: it was the center of trade to the West Indies and the seat of the Casa de Contratación, which managed that trade, and it also contained a little group of English merchants, mostly from Bristol. Of this coterie the leader was the younger Robert Thorne, whose father had earlier backed John Cabot, so that when Sebastian took up his duties he found himself in familiar company. Thorne had followed Spain's voyages with interest, even to the point of investing money in them, and he was to write in 1527 a memorial for Henry VIII advocating the Northwest Passage as a gateway to Asia. Though this paper long remained in manuscript, to be published by Richard Hakluyt in 1582, it is known that in the interim the thesis was widely circulated and had much influence.

This little circle of Bristolians formed the chief means of carrying information from Spain to England of the doings of the Conquistadores in the West Indies and the Spanish Main. By virtue of living in Seville these men learned as much as anyone could about the Spanish conquests in the New World. In fact, they actually took part in one voyage of discovery when, in 1526, Thorne financed an expedition (flying the Spanish flag, of course) that was to seek a passage to India through the Plate estuary and sail on to the mythical lands of Ophir and Tarsis. Sebastian Cabot was the admiral and with him were several of the Bristol-Seville merchants—Henry Latimer, the pilot, and Roger Barlow, the supercargo—so that the venture had a distinctly Tudor character. They found, of course, that the Plate was a dead end, but they sailed a thousand miles upstream, right to Paraguay, and here learned by hearsay of the silver mines of Peru that later brought the conquering Pizarro.

Cabot's party returned to Spain in 1529, leaving only a fort (above present-day Rosario), long known as Gaboto's Fort, a landmark in that flat country. As for Cabot, he stayed on in Spanish service at least until 1544. The date of his return to England is unknown, but he was back in Bristol by 1547 with the greatest stock of geographical knowledge possessed by any man in the realm.

As for England itself during the first half of the century, there is little enough to tell. Henry VIII was only intermittently interested in discovery. He sponsored ineffective projects in 1516 and 1521, and the two later expeditions which reached America, John Rut's in 1527 (which coasted eastern North America and reached the West Indies) and Richard Hore's in 1536, were not of much significance. Henry's chief contribution, though indirect, was of far-reaching effect. His founding of the Tudor navy made possible not only Elizabeth's victory in the Spanish War but also much of the later progress of discovery and colonization.

The repute of certain voyages led by the original William Hawkins of Plymouth may be said to have placed the stamp of Devonshire on Tudor seafaring. In 1530 this progenitor of a famous brood sailed to the Grain Coast of West Africa, took on a load of ivory, crossed to Brazil, and returned home with a Brazilian "king" whom he presented to Henry VIII at Whitehall. Ten years later he repeated the triangle, lading "elephants' teeth" in Africa and brazilwood on this side of the Atlantic. There is also evidence of voyages from Southampton along the same route during these years, even though there was still no sign of a national awakening to the possibilities of transoceanic commerce such as had long been observable in Spain and Portugal. For this upsurge of a nationwide effort England had to wait for mid-century.

The convenient year 1550 may be said to mark the beginning of English travel and discovery as a national interest, as well as the date at which England entered the field as a competitor of the two original colonial powers, Spain and Portugal. The voyages of Cabot and Hawkins were all rather haphazard and

IOANNES HAWKINS

Aduancement by diligence

Qui vicit toties ins fructis classibus hostes
Ille vagis HAVKINS vitam relliquit in Vndis

Plate 2. Sir John Hawkins (1532–1595). Led three slaving voyages to Africa and West Indies, culminating in tragedy of San Juan de Ulúa (1569). Brilliant administrator (treasurer and comptroller) of Navy from 1573. Served against Armada; died off Puerto Rico while on Drake's last voyage (1595). From Henry Holland, *Herwologia* (1620).

sporadic enterprises, and they had no immediate results—at least on a national scale.

By contrast, since the first Tudor had come to the throne the Portuguese had rounded the Cape of Good Hope, established themselves in India, and planted their flag as far afield as the Spice Islands and China; and they were conducting with clockwork regularity a thoroughly formalized annual trade between Lisbon, Goa, and Malacca. During the same period the Spaniards had explored and settled the West Indies, conquered Mexico and Peru, and under Magellan had successfully sent an expedition around the globe. To this revolutionary progress of world discovery, England's only contribution had been an indirect result of the Cabot voyages—the revealing of the highly profitable codfish grounds off the Grand Banks.

During much of Edward VI's reign, however, there were several influential personalities in England whose aim it was to further voyaging as a truly British interest, with the particular goal of finding a safe and satisfactory seaway to the Orient. Noteworthy among these was old Sebastian Cabot, back again in what he patriotically considered his native country, with a mass of experience second to none. Associated with him was John Dee, a young Welshman of brilliant erudition, whose dealing with the occult soon gave rise to the suspicion that he was in league with the powers of darkness. And as their patron, who gave their plans the backing of the highest authority, they had no less a personage than John Dudley, Earl of Warwick (created Duke of Northumberland in 1551), who was the real ruler of England during Edward VI's minority. Northumberland has gone down in history as a somber and sinister figure, with many black marks against him; but before we condemn him out of hand we should remember that it was his support and encouragement that made the voyages of the early 1550's possible and thereby started the subsequent Elizabethan expansion.

As a result of the pleading and influence of these men and others of their circle the mercantile community of London and

Bristol became interested in the possibilities of overseas enterprise, especially as furthering the sale of England's chief export—woolen cloth. A syndicate formed in 1553 to exploit the Northeast Passage to China later became the earliest of the great joint-stock companies, "The Merchant Adventurers of England for the Discovery of Lands, Territories, Isles, Dominions, and Seignories Unknown," otherwise the Muscovy or Russia Company (chartered in 1555). Simultaneously several magnates in the City became attracted by the prospect of trade with Barbary and West Africa. Thus at its mid-century inception English enterprise was aimed in two directions: northeast around the North Cape to Russia and the Orient; and southwest to Africa, the Spanish Main, and eventually the Pacific Ocean.

In 1551 Thomas Wyndham, a Somerset aristocrat and a protégé of Northumberland's, with, however, well-developed predatory instincts of his own when on the high seas, made a very profitable venture to the Barbary Coast of Morocco, thereby starting the sequence of voyages in that direction. This success led him to make a second expedition to Barbary (1552), which in turn emboldened him to a still wider extension of his activities. In 1553 he sailed to Guinea itself, raiding and plundering on the way, but nevertheless amassing a considerable cargo of gold dust. However, he reached Benin during the worst of the hot season, and the deadly climate of the Oil Rivers killed him and most of his crew. Only just enough men were left to work his ships, which regained England after much hardship to win a handsome profit from the gold. This evidence of the profits to be won in such adventures led to a succession of annual voyages to the Barbary Coast throughout the 1550's. These expeditions (with strong financial support in the City of London) by sailing earlier in the season and keeping west of the Portuguese fort of Elmina were able to show a continual profit from gold, ivory, and pepper with a relatively small loss of crew. In these undertakings the most successful captain was William Towerson, who commanded three ven-

Plate 3. Sir Martin Frobisher (1535–1594). Served in West African voyages in 1550's. Made three voyages in search of Northwest Passage (1576–1578). Served brilliantly against Armada. From Henry Holland, *Herwologia* (1620).

tures, and it was in them that young Martin Frobisher first played his part on the stage of naval history.

These profitable West African voyages continued far into the next decade, when they developed from mere trading enterprises to the Gold Coast into slaving voyages sailing from England to Guinea and thence across the Atlantic to the Spanish Main. Such was the genesis of the celebrated "triangle trade," which was to be such a source of profit to our eighteenth-century ancestors. In this development John Hawkins of Plymouth, son of old William, played a leading role, and here his young cousin Francis Drake received the rudiments of his nautical education. Even though England and Spain were at peace in that period and ostensibly friendly, the slave trade to the Spanish colonies was strictly forbidden to foreigners under heavy penalties. Still, so great was the demand for slave labor that a little collusion with the authorities enabled the English to reap substantial profits from this commerce.

Hawkins made three voyages on the "triangle." His first (1562–1563) and his second (1564–1565) were alike successful —so successful in fact that the anger of the Spanish government at the illegal intrusion of this Lutheran interloper was thoroughly aroused. Both times, after taking on his cargo at Sierra Leone, Hawkins had led an English fleet across to the Caribbean and sold his slaves at ports in Venezuela and Colombia, as well as in the larger islands. In doing so he had openly defied the dictates of His Most Christian Majesty, and in consequence, when Hawkins reached the Spanish Main on his "third troublesome voyage" (1568) he found quite a different reception awaiting him, the authorities everywhere hostile and defiant. After several exasperating months on the coast, Hawkins sailed to San Juan de Ulúa, a small harbor near Vera Cruz in Mexico. He had not quite started to careen when the Spanish plate fleet hove in sight, vastly outnumbering his crippled armament. This put Hawkins in a very tight spot, but he was able to make an agreement with the Spanish commander, enabling him to get on with the job of refitting and victualing. The Spaniard, however, had no intention of abiding by the agreement; he treacherously opened fire on Hawkins and pretty well blew his ships out of the water. With luck and good seamanship, Hawkins in the "Minion" and Francis Drake in the "Judith" made their escape and struggled back to England with a few survivors to tell the tale of Spanish treachery.

In its political results the disaster of San Juan de Ulúa was far-reaching indeed, for it ended all hope of English trade in the West Indies, besides making a definite break in the long period of Anglo-Spanish good will and commercial relations that had endured since Henry VII. As such it was a definite turning point, for the infamy of the Spaniards was never forgiven by the subjects of Elizabeth, and henceforth there was "no peace beyond the Line," that is, the prime meridian through the Azores, and the latitude line of the Tropic of Cancer. The first step along the path to the Armada of '88 had been taken.

For Hawkins' successor, the brilliant and fiery Francis Drake, this event was the signal for a jihad, and he determined to carry fire and sword to the Spanish colonies, whatever the official relations of his country with Spain. In 1571 he made his first independent cruise to the Spanish Main, where he reconnoitered the Isthmus of Panama—the strategic bottleneck through which all treasure from Peru had to pass. Next year he was back on the same coast and out for blood, and after many vicissitudes he pulled off the daring coup of capturing a great convoy of silver and other treasure as it was crossing the Isthmus. Elizabeth was naturally embarrassed on Drake's return and sought to disavow the episode. Drake himself discreetly went into hiding for a couple of years — to plan his greatest and most celebrated venture.

Drake's voyage of circumnavigation is far and away the most famous of all Tudor voyages, not only because of its fabulously profitable results, but also because it caught the imagination of Englishmen then and has held it ever since. Its purposes appear to have been threefold: to find a seaway to the Orient by the Strait of Magellan and the Pacific, to look for the southern

Plate 4. Sir Walter Raleigh (1552–1618). Founded unsuccessful
Roanoke colony. Explored Guiana (1595). Served at capture of
Cadiz (1596) and in "Islands Voyage" to Azores (1597). Im-
prisoned on accession of James I but released in 1616 in order to
find gold mines of Guiana. This expedition failed and he was
executed on Tower Hill. Portrait by an unknown artist, 1588;
courtesy of the National Portrait Gallery, London.

continent of Terra Australis (a favorite concept of John Dee's), and to pay expenses by preying on Spanish shipping in the Pacific—this latter plan being known only to Drake himself and the Queen. Burghley, the Queen's chief counselor, knew nothing whatever about the voyage, while the crews were shipped for a trading expedition to the Mediterranean. Plans and preparations for the undertaking were indeed "top secret."

It was against this background that Drake sailed from Plymouth in the fall of 1577 with three ships and two smaller vessels, having among his company William Hawkins III (John's nephew); John Winter, an excellent sailor, whose reputation, however, suffered from his abandoning of the voyage off the Strait; and Thomas Doughty, a courtier and a landsman, who was a disciple of John Dee and was therefore suspected of traffic in necromancy. This sinister figure was from the start a thorn in Drake's side, and by the time the fleet had arrived below the Plate estuary some believed that Doughty had been practicing witchcraft in order to hinder the voyage. At Port St. Julian on the remote Patagonian coast, where Magellan had endured rebellion and hardship sixty years earlier, Doughty was tried and executed for conjuring and incitement to mutiny. Drake's methods were no doubt summary, but the discipline of the voyage was preserved.

Indeed Drake needed all the discipline he could enforce, for his passage around South America was a terrifying experience. Having negotiated the Strait without too much trouble, he met a series of frightful storms off the western mouth: Winter in the "Elizabeth" parted company and made his way back to England; the "Marigold" went down with all hands; and Drake in the "Pelican" (now renamed the "Golden Hind") was driven eastward far south of the Horn. This mishap led to an important discovery, for the mythical land mass of the southern continent was shown to be open sea and as such appeared in the greatest of Tudor maps, the Wright-Molyneux Map of 1600. Eventually Drake succeeded in regaining the Pacific and sailed north along the coasts of Chile and Peru, picking up unsuspecting

Spanish craft on the way. His capture of the great galleon "Cacafuego," with her fabulous cargo of Peruvian silver, "made" the voyage many times over. After that Drake steered northward to get out of Spanish waters and to explore the western outlet of the Northwest Passage, or the Straits of Anian, as Dee called it.

This course brought him to Drake's Bay, where he wintered. Its precise location is still a matter of acrimonious dispute among native-son Californians (and others), but it undoubtedly was in the vicinity of San Francisco. Having decided that the Straits of Anian did not exist, at least in those latitudes, Drake bore away across the broad Pacific to Ternate in the Moluccas, where he made a cordial treaty with the local sultan and took on a good lading of cloves. His course then lay to the south of Java, where he nearly came to grief on a submerged rock, across the Indian Ocean to the Cape, and thence back to England, which he reached in September, 1580, with a wonderfully rich cargo. His venture was indeed a brilliant financial success, and he brought back treasures beyond his wildest hopes.

To explain away Drake's voyage to Philip of Spain required some clever diplomacy on the part of Queen Elizabeth. But actual war between the two nations was getting ever nearer, and in 1585 Drake led a large expedition to Spanish possessions in the Atlantic islands and the West Indies. After first raiding Santiago in the Cape Verdes, he sailed across the ocean, stormed Santo Domingo, Cartagena in Colombia, and St. Augustine in Florida, and then called at the Carolina coast in June, 1586, to take home the survivors of Raleigh's first Roanoke colony. It was a memorable voyage, but rather a part of the Spanish War than of the story of exploration.

A second circumnavigation was made during this period by Thomas Cavendish, a veteran of Grenville's voyage to Roanoke. Cavendish's venture requires little description, for it was the speediest and least eventful of all the early circumnavigations. Sailing in 1586 and closely following Drake's track, he passed

14

Plate 5. Drake at Cartagena (1585). This plate shows the daring attack of English troops, supported by the fleet, on the powerful Spanish fortress on the coast of present-day Colombia. It resulted in the capture of one of Spain's strongest points in America. From Theodor de Bry, *America* (1595).

the Strait successfully and off Mexico made his big prize of a homeward-bound galleon from Manila, crammed with Oriental goods of great value. Having no further reason for delay, Cavendish steered for England by way of the Cape and reached home in September, 1588—just after the Armada had been dispersed. Emboldened by this success and deciding to tempt Providence a second time, Cavendish set out in 1591 with Captain John Davis, the famous Arctic navigator. But his luck did not hold: he met with extremely violent weather in the Strait, was driven back into the Atlantic, and was lost with his ship at sea off St. Helena. In the remaining vessel Davis managed to get back to England, to pursue a distinguished career as sailor and nautical expert until his death at the hands of Japanese pirates off Singapore twelve years later.

In 1553 the group which later formed the Muscovy Company under the stimulus of the Duke of Northumberland, Sebastian Cabot, and John Dee sent out an expedition of three ships, commanded by Sir Hugh Willoughby, with instructions to reach China by the Northeast Passage. Both failure and success awaited the venture: failure in that China was never reached, success in that Russia was fortuitously gained instead. A storm off the North Cape separated the ships, and Willoughby was forced to winter in north Norway, where he perished with all his crew. His second-in-command, Richard Chancellor, meanwhile sailed his ship through the White Sea to Archangel and then journeyed south to Moscow, where he was well received by Ivan the Terrible. Russia, which hitherto had access to the West solely by overland trade routes controlled by the Hanseatic League, was most fortunate to have English vessels open up a northern outlet, and the Czar was therefore well pleased to grant liberal trading privileges to the "Merchant Venturers." Chancellor returned to England in the summer of 1554, not indeed having reached Cathay, but having performed a substantial service nonetheless. Making a second visit to Russia in 1555–1556, Chancellor was drowned on his return voyage, but a distinguished passenger, Ivan's ambassador to Queen Elizabeth's court, arrived in London as the first representative of his nation to be seen there.

Because of these developments, the original purpose of the "Merchant Venturers" became somewhat deflected; trade with Russia became its main interest, and even its name was altered in common use to "the Muscovy Company." Nevertheless, the search for the Passage was not wholly forgotten, for in 1556 an expedition under Stephen Borough set forth from the Thames with that objective. We are left with a charming picture of old Sebastian Cabot, who traveled down to Gravesend to wish the party godspeed; the "good old gentleman" inspected the vessel, dined with the crew at the Christopher Inn, and then took part in the dance that followed. Borough made a valiant attempt to do the impossible and turned back only when stopped by pack ice in the Kara Sea off Siberia; he must indeed have considered himself lucky to have returned alive to England. But by this time two of the principal advocates of the Passage had died: Northumberland on the scaffold after Mary's accession to the throne in 1553, and Cabot, the grand old figure whose sixty years of activity linked the days of Columbus with those of Queen Elizabeth, in 1557. The prime movers of the search gone, no further attempt at the Northeast Passage was made until 1580, when Arthur Pet and Charles Jackman sailed at Dee's instigation, to be barred again by the icy barrier of the Kara Sea.

If the Passage itself was out of the picture, the overland road across Russia still gave promise of a highway to the Orient, and it was not long before imaginative Britons began to consider the possibilities thereof. As a result, several of the most interesting journeys in the annals of English travel were performed. First of the daring pioneers who traveled into Central Asia was an employee of the Muscovy Company named Anthony Jenkinson, who led a small party of English down the Volga in the spring of 1558, sailed across the Caspian with the red cross flag of England at the masthead, and then made his

17

way across Turkestan by caravan to Bokhara. After a winter spent in fruitless negotiations with the local Emir, Jenkinson became convinced that there was no prospect of trade with either India or China in that quarter, and in consequence he and his colleagues made their weary way back to Moscow.

A second journey took the intrepid Jenkinson once more across the Caspian to Derbent in the Caucasus (1561), where the Briton was well received by a friendly governor named Abdullah Khan. From Derbent, Jenkinson made his way overland to Kazvin, where the reigning monarch of Persia, Shah Tahmasp, had his capital. His reception by the Sophy was cool and Jenkinson came away with no trading privileges whatever. On his return, however, he made a favorable arrangement with Abdullah Khan by which English woolens were to be exchanged for Persian silk. Thus was established what was for a time an active trade, and English parties continued to travel across the Caspian to Persia and Georgia. But the premature death of Abdullah Khan, together with the simultaneous incursion of the Turks into the Caucasus region, put an end to this promising commerce, while further expeditions to Persia itself were prevented by the fickleness of the Shah, by continued epidemics of the plague, and by the hazards of Caspian navigation. A final expedition, led by Arthur Edwards in 1579, convinced the Britons that the game was not worth the candle: the distances were too great, the hardships were too extreme, and latterly the Turkish peril was too menacing. As one of Edwards' colleagues realistically put it after a mission to Persia: "Better it is in my opinion to continue a beggar in England during life than to remain a rich merchant seven years in this country." Like the Northeast Passage, the trans-Caspian route to India and Cathay had indeed come to a dead end.

In England, however, men were still sanguine about a seaway to the Orient, and even if the track around the North Cape had been proved futile, there were great expectations in some quarters for the Northwest Passage to the north of North America. Foremost of the advocates of this road was the ir-

Plate 6. Drake at the River Plate (1578). An incident during the famous circumnavigation. Drake and a shore party are greeted by playful Indians, who steal the admiral's hat. A vessel is being careened in the background. From Theodor de Bry, *America* (1595).

repressible magician John Dee, and allied with him in this interest was the Devonshire squire Sir Humphrey Gilbert, the elder half brother of Sir Walter Raleigh. In fact Gilbert had composed an enthusiastic treatise on the Passage, which circulated in manuscript for a decade before appearing in 1576 as *A Discourse of a Discovery for a New Passage to Cataia*. In brief, the theory of the Passage was that beyond Labrador there was open water running southwest through the Straits of Anian into the Pacific, and that the land to the north of the Straits was part of continental Asia. Dee and Gilbert built up such a convincing case for the Passage that large financial assistance for the scheme was forthcoming in London, especially from the Lok family, who had been so active in the West African trade of the 1550's. Because of this, it was only natural that the leader of the expedition, Martin Frobisher, should have been a man experienced on the Guinea Coast, albeit his more recent service had included flagrant acts of piracy in home waters.

Frobisher made three voyages in search of the Passage in three successive years (1576, '77, '78). On his first trip he reached Frobisher's Strait in Baffin Land—actually not a strait at all but a cul-de-sac (now known as Frobisher Bay). Here he found a rock outcrop rich in mica, which to him and others of his party appeared to be rich gold. This find had the effect of wholly deflecting the enterprise, and Frobisher loaded his ships and sailed home with a cargo of very questionable minerals. As a result, the quest for the Passage degenerated into a bucketshop mining venture, and on his next voyage Frobisher barely made even a token gesture of looking for the Passage; instead he loaded his vessels in the Strait and went right back to England. It was at least with the virtue of frankness, therefore, that Frobisher set out on the third expedition, as the Passage had been completely forgotten about by that time and the sole purpose of the venture was loading ore. Nevertheless, this voyage did result in an advance of exploration, as Frobisher in heavy weather lost his bearings and fortuitously penetrated two

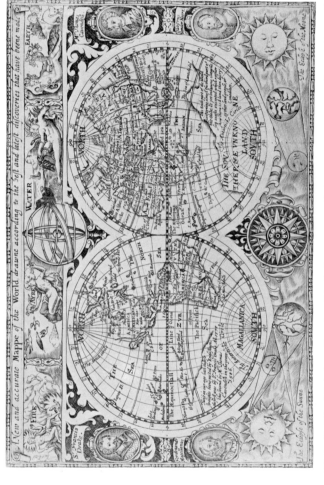

Plate 7. World map, showing Drake's voyage of circumnavigation. This is from the first independent version of Drake's narrative, which was published in London in 1628 as *The World Encompassed.* The mysterious Southern Continent may be seen on the map; at the sides are the four early circumnavigators—Magellan, Drake, Cavendish, and Van Noort; above are the four elements and an armillary sphere.

hundred miles into Hudson Strait, which he rightly concluded was a potential seaway to China. Frobisher then turned back to load his fool's gold and sailed away to England to find that the ore had been pronounced worthless. The bubble had burst, the company was bankrupt, and Lok was in a debtors' prison. So ended ignominiously the second round in the quest for the Northwest Passage.

With Lok in jail, Gilbert drowned, and Dee gone to practice his black arts in Bohemia, the chief backers of the Passage were out of the picture by 1584; yet interest was still keen, and in place of the original patrons appeared Sir Francis Walsingham, William Sanderson (a wealthy citizen of London), and Gilbert's half brother, Sir Walter Raleigh. This group selected John Davis of Dartmouth, in Devon, as commander, a sailor of both practical and theoretical skill, whose long career on the seven seas places him in the front rank of Tudor mariners.

Like Frobisher, Davis made three voyages in as many years (1585, '86, '87), but unlike his predecessor he did not allow himself to be diverted by a will-o'-the-wisp of a gold mine. His ventures were actuated solely by his desire to find a passage to China, and to this end he sailed far to the north of Frobisher's track, in the open water between Greenland and Baffin Land. His first voyage took him to Gilbert Sound on the west coast of Greenland, named in honor of Sir Humphrey; his second venture revealed Cumberland Sound (christened for the Earl of Cumberland) in Baffin Land; and his third expedition reached the very high latitude of 72° N, where Davis named a mountainous headland Sanderson's Hope as a gesture to his wealthy backer. Davis had by no means negotiated the Passage, but he had found the only practicable way to it, for from this latitude the course led west through Melville Sound and the Beaufort Sea to Bering Strait, the track followed by Amundsen when he made the first traverse of the Passage in 1903–1905. How far Davis himself might have gone if events had permitted the continuation of the enterprise is an open question, but when he returned to England in 1587 the Spanish Armada was already in the making and Davis' talents were needed for sterner duties in home waters.

Nevertheless, despite the intervention of the Spanish War and the subsequent development of the southeastern route to India, interest in the Northwest Passage persisted far into the next century. In 1610–1611 Henry Hudson sailed through Hudson Strait into Hudson Bay, which he explored in the hope of finding a channel into the Pacific. His ship, the "Discovery," became icebound, however, and he was forced to spend a winter of great hardship. The crew mutinied and set the great explorer adrift in an open boat in the icy waters of the bay that bears his name. In 1616 Robert Bylot and William Baffin sailed through Baffin Bay and actually reached the latitude of 78° N, hardly eight hundred miles from the Pole—a point not passed until the days of Sir John Franklin in the last century. In 1631 two separate expeditions, led by Luke Fox and Thomas James respectively, sought to solve the riddle of the north-western exit of Hudson Bay and thus discovered James Bay. Such is the roster of the northwestern voyages in the Tudor and Stuart periods, which, if they led to no other result, at least bore fruit in the creation of the highly successful Hudson's Bay Company by Prince Rupert in 1670.

From 1587 until 1604 a state of war existed between England and Spain, and although hostilities at sea played themselves out during the final years of the conflict, the first decade of the struggle witnessed almost continual naval warfare, in which all the celebrated sailors of the day bore distinguished parts. Drake had indeed been fighting Spain on his own since the fatal day at San Juan de Ulúa, and his large-scale campaign in the West Indies in 1585–1586 was in a very real sense an integral part of the war that was to follow. His aggressive strategy was thus not affected by the *de jure* creation of a state of hostilities, and he simply went on pursuing his own course. To a lesser degree the same was true of his colleagues, so that

Plate 8. A view showing the arrival of English ships off Hatteras and the approach of settlers to Roanoke Island. Already Hatteras had a bad reputation for storms, and five wrecked ships are shown in the foreground. From Thomas Harriot's *Brief and True Report* (1590).

the transition of Elizabeth's navy from a peacetime basis to a wartime one was so slight as to pass unnoticed.

Drake's first voyage after the actual outbreak of hostilities was his attack on Cadiz in 1587, when he "singed the King of Spain's beard" by sailing boldly into Cadiz harbor and sinking and burning all the shipping that lay within reach. This had the effect of upsetting Philip's preparations for the Armada. Even more portentous was Drake's capture of the Cape of Sagres in extreme southwestern Portugal, where Henry the Navigator had had his headquarters a century and a half before. In the ensuing year, the famous '88, the Armada made its attack on England—an episode too well known in history to be rehearsed here and only indirectly related to Tudor voyaging. But in 1589 Drake and Norris made their campaign against Lisbon, penetrating into the Tagus estuary but failing to capture the Portuguese capital. A more extensive campaigning voyage was that of Lord Thomas Howard to the Azores in 1591, immortalized for all time by the superb heroism of Sir Richard Grenville in the "Revenge," who fought a single-ship action against tremendous odds—with the inevitable result. And in these years, too, from 1586 to 1598, the Earl of Cumberland—that hardy perennial of Elizabethan naval ventures—made no less than ten privateering voyages, almost one each year. These expeditions (none save the last notably successful) extended from West Africa to the West Indies, with the Atlantic Islands as the center of attraction. In his final voyage of 1598, however, Cumberland made a noteworthy sack of San Juan in Puerto Rico which went far towards redressing his previous failures.

In 1593 Richard Hawkins, the only son of Sir John, sailed on a privateering cruise by which he hoped to reach China and the East Indies and to make expenses by raiding Spanish shipping on the way. His course took him through the Strait of Magellan, his being the third English fleet (after those of Drake and Cavendish) to make the passage. Entering the Pacific, he turned north along the coast, plundering as he went; but as a result of the depredations of his predecessors the Spaniards were well prepared and Hawkins was brought to bay off Ecuador. His ship, the "Dainty," surrendered when in a sinking condition after a hammer-and-tongs battle of three whole days; Hawkins was wounded six times and was carried off in apparently a dying condition. Yet he lived to serve many years of imprisonment in both South America and Spain, eventually returning to his native Devonshire and seeing his last action against the Algerian pirates in 1620–1621.

Transoceanic voyages of a belligerent character were indeed of more than an annual occurrence during these years. In 1595 James Lancaster, just returned from the first English voyage to the East Indies by the Cape of Good Hope route, led an expedition to Brazil, where he sacked Pernambuco. In the same year Drake and Sir John Hawkins, shipmates of the voyage to San Juan de Ulúa so many years before, made their final cruise to the West Indies. It was a complete failure: Puerto Rico was attacked in vain and Hawkins died off San Juan; Drake then took the fleet to Panama, only to die himself off Porto Bello; and in the teeth of Spanish attacks the fleet was brought home by Sir Thomas Baskerville, a soldier and a landsman, who nonetheless executed a most difficult assignment with remarkable skill.

A British success, however transitory, may be recorded for the following year, 1596, when Sir Thomas Sherley, a picturesque adventurer whose later career was to be associated with Persia and Spain, led a fleet to Jamaica and occupied the island in the name of Queen Elizabeth. But he left no force to continue the occupation, and as soon as he had sailed away the inhabitants quite properly transferred their allegiance back to Philip of Spain.

Nearer home, however, the same year brought a brilliant and lasting success, almost rivaling the defeat of the Armada as the great event of the Spanish War—the sack of Cadiz by the forces of Sir Walter Raleigh and the Earl of Essex. This

THE PRINCIPALL
NAVIGATIONS, VOIA-
GES AND DISCOVERIES OF THE
English nation, made by Sea or ouer Land,
to the most remote and farthest distant Quarters of
the earth at any time within the compasse
of these 1500. yeeres : Deuided into three
seuerall parts, according to the po-
sitions of the Regions whereunto they were directed.

The first, conteining the personall trauels of the English vnto *Iudæa, Syria, A-rabia,* the riuer *Euphrates, Babylon, Balsara,* the *Persian* Gulfe, *Ormuz, Chaul, Goa, India,* and many Ilands adioyning to the South parts of *Asia :* toge-ther with the like vnto *Egypt,* the chiefest ports and places of *Africa* with-in and without the Streight of *Gibraltar,* and about the famous Promon-torie of *Buona Esperança.*

The second, comprehending the worthy discoueries of the English towards the North and Northeast by Sea, as of *Lapland, Scrikfinia, Corelia,* the Baie of *S. Nicholas,* the Isles of *Colgoieue, Vaigats,* and *Noua Zembla* toward the great riuer *Ob,* with the mightie Empire of *Russia,* the *Caspian* Sea, *Georgia, Armenia, Media, Persia, Boghar* in *Bactria,* & diuers kingdoms of *Tartaria.*

The third and last, including the English valiant attempts in searching al-most all the corners of the vaste and new world of *America,* from 73. de-grees of Northerly latitude Southward, to *Meta Incognita, Newfoundland,* the maine ot *Virginia,* the point of *Florida,* the Baie of *Mexico,* all the In-land of *Noua Hispania,* the coast of *Terra firma, Brasill,* the riuer of *Plate,* to the Streight of *Magellan :* and through it, and from it in the South Sea to *Chili, Peru, Xalisco,* the Gulfe of *California, Noua Albion* vpon the backside of *Canada,* further then euer any Christian hitherto hath pierced.

Whereunto is added the last most renowmed English Nauigation,
round about the whole Globe of the Earth.

By *Richard Hakluyt* Master of Artes, and Student sometime
of Christ-church in Oxford.

Imprinted at London by GEORGE BISHOP
and RALPH NEWBERIE, Deputies to
CHRISTOPHER BARKER, Printer to the
Queenes most excellent Maiestie.

1589.

Plate 9. The title page of the first edition of Hakluyt's *Voyages,* which appeared in one volume in London in 1589. The second and better-known edition came out in three volumes, 1598–1600. The monumental work on Tudor voyaging has been rightly called "the prose epic of the English Nation" (James Anthony Froude).

was a far more substantial venture than Drake's attack on the same town in 1587, for after the defeat of the Armada Philip sought to regain maritime supremacy by building a dozen of the greatest warships afloat, "The Twelve Apostles." Most of these giants were caught in harbor by Essex and Raleigh and utterly destroyed, along with Philip's hopes of ever beating England at sea. Besides this, the city of Cadiz, the principal entrepôt for the trade of the Indies, was sacked, occupied for some days, and then burnt. It was a body blow to Philip's war effort.

In 1597 the Raleigh-Essex team was out again with a large fleet on what is known to history as "The Islands Voyage." This was a cruise in Azorean waters in the hope of nabbing the annual plate fleet on its way from Panama to Cadiz. Bad luck dogged the English: the great prize was missed and only a few individual ships were taken. Furthermore, when the fleet returned to England they were greeted with the alarming intelligence that the Spaniards had been raiding the Cornish coast in their absence.

With the humiliating return of the Islands Voyage in 1597 and the far more jubilant homecoming of the Earl of Cumberland from Puerto Rico the following year, active campaigning voyages came virtually to an end for the remainder of the war, to be supplanted by land warfare in Ireland and the Netherlands. It is time, then, to examine briefly two colonial enterprises of the war years, each of which was associated with the name of Sir Walter Raleigh.

It was probably through his half brother, Sir Humphrey Gilbert, that Raleigh became interested in planting a colony of Englishmen in North America. Gilbert, an unwavering backer of Frobisher and the Northwest Passage, had planned a settlement on the North American mainland. After a nominal annexation of Newfoundland in 1583, he pushed on to find a mainland site for a colony but was forced to turn back towards England and was drowned on the way home. In the next year, however, Richard Hakluyt penned his powerful plea for American colonization in the "Discourse concerning Western Planting." Raleigh simultaneously renewed his dead brother's patent for colonization and sent his captains, Arthur Barlow and Philip Amadas, on a coastal reconnaissance of the land named in honor of Elizabeth—Virginia. These men passed through the inlet above Cape Hatteras and thus discovered Roanoke Island, which seemed an excellent site for a settlement.

In the following year, 1585, Raleigh sent out his first colonizing party under the command of Sir Richard Grenville (of the "Revenge"). With him were Ralph Lane, the chief political figure of the colonists; Thomas Cavendish, the circumnavigator; Thomas Harriot, a brilliant mathematician and freethinker, to whose pen we owe the history of the settlement; and John White, whose delicate water colors of the Carolina Low Country are among the most precious documents of early Americana (preserved in the British Museum). A village was built on Roanoke Island and some exploration was carried out in Albemarle and Pamlico Sounds; but after a year Lane and his men realized that they were in a hostile land with very little to eat. In this crisis they were fortuitously delivered by Sir Francis Drake, homeward bound from his great raid in the West Indies, whose offer to repatriate the colonists was accepted with the greatest enthusiasm.

Two years later, 1587, Raleigh sent out his second supply of colonists to Roanoke led by John White and including a number of women. White returned to England for more equipment shortly thereafter, bringing hopeful tidings of the colony; but by this time the Spanish War was in full swing, with the Armada in the making, so that it was not until 1590 that affairs had become sufficiently settled for White to find transport to bring him back to Roanoke. This was the final tragedy of the "Lost Colony." White reached the coast amid the perils of a Hatteras tempest which made a thorough search impossible; but in any event no colonists were found, nor any trace of them save the cryptic word "Croatoan" carved on a tree.

A briefe and true report
of the new found land of Virginia.
of the commodities and of the nature and man
ners of the naturall inhabitants. Discouered by
the English Colony there seated by Sir Richard
Greinuile Knight In the yere 1585. Which Rema
ined Vnder the gouernement of twelue monethes,
At the speciall charge and direction of the Honou
rable Sir WALTER RALEIGH Knight lord Warden
of the stannereis Who therein hath beene fauoured
and authorised by her MAIESTIE
:and her letters patents:
This fore booke Is made in English
BY Thomas Hariot seruant to the abouenamed
Sir WALTER, a member of the Colony, and there
imployed in discouering

CVM GRATIA ET PRIVILEGIO CÆS.MA.TIS SPECIA.LI

FRANCOFORTI AD MOENVM
TIPIS IOANNIS WECHELI, SVMTIBVS VERO THEODORI
DE BRY ANNO CIƆ IƆ XC.
VENALES REPERIVNTVR IN OFFICINA SIGISMVNDI FEIRABENDII

Plate 10. The account of Raleigh's Roanoke colony by Thomas Harriot, a distinguished mathematician, who accompanied the expedition. The plates were copied from water color drawings made on the spot by John White, a capable artist. The originals are now in the British Museum.

Nothing else has survived of Raleigh's Virginia experiment save a vast amount of hypothesis and speculation.

If Raleigh was beaten in Virginia, however, he soon had hopes of the possibilities of another part of America. From the days of the Conquistadores in the first half of the century there had been a persistent legend of the fabled realm of El Dorado in the northeastern part of South America, where in the golden city of Manoa on the Lake of Parima the gilded monarch known as El Dorado ruled a kingdom of unparalleled splendor. A Spanish captain named Berrio had explored the Orinoco valley and had reached Trinidad after a transcontinental journey of great hardship, with high expectations of finding the Gilded Man. One of Raleigh's captains captured at sea in 1594 a full report to the Spanish government from Domingo de Vera, Berrio's lieutenant, so that the ever-sanguine Sir Walter was able to get the latest news of the fabled country. This was enough for Raleigh, who soon organized an expedition and was off to Guiana in 1595. Landing at Trinidad, he had the fortune to capture Berrio himself, who so filled the credulous Briton with misinformation that Raleigh and his men were soon on their way up the Orinoco in small boats, heading for the golden city of Manoa. His adventure was short-lived, however, for a waterfall blocked his way when he tried to gain the Promised Land by a side river (the Caroni), and he got back to the Orinoco to find it in high flood. So it fell out that the wet and weary Englishmen made their way to Trinidad and shortly afterwards sailed back home. Next year, nevertheless, Raleigh sent out a second expedition under his friend and captain, Lawrence Keymis, and this voyage resulted in considerably more geographical knowledge, for Keymis made a detailed survey of the rivers of Guiana and concluded that the Essequibo was the outlet of Lake Parima. There is some indication that Raleigh had colonial settlement in mind in sending this voyage, but whatever his motives El Dorado remained as far away as ever.

With the passing of Elizabeth and the accession of James, Raleigh's already declining power at court quite collapsed. He was sent to the Tower, and the El Dorado myth began to fade. However, sufficient reconnaissance had been made to suggest Guiana as an overseas settlement for Englishmen, and in 1604 Captain Charles Leigh started a colony on the present-day border of Cayenne and Surinam. This was a complete failure within a year, but a relief party under the leader's brother, Sir Oliph Leigh, took formal possession of the island of Barbados in the name of King James. Further vain attempts to settle Guiana were made by Robert Harcourt in 1609 and 1613 and by Roger North in 1620.

Meanwhile, Raleigh had been released from his imprisonment to make his second expedition to Guiana in 1617—his swan song in the quest for El Dorado. His river party on the Orinoco ran head on into the Spanish fort upstream; Sir Walter's son was killed, and Captain Keymis, who had led the party astray, committed suicide after telling Raleigh of the failure. Raleigh thereupon sailed back to England—to meet his end on Tower Hill.

This tragedy, together with the failure of Roger North's colony in 1620, caused the promoters in London to look to the Lesser Antilles for settlement rather than to the Guiana mainland. In 1622 Thomas Warner, one of North's old companions, voyaged to the Sugar Islands. His selection of a site for a colony fell on the island of St. Christopher (St. Kitts), and having reported favorably in London, he went back two years later (1624) to establish the first permanent English settlement in the West Indies. The success of his colony led to an even more prosperous settlement in Barbados in 1627 by John and Henry Powell. Nevis was colonized in 1628, and Antigua and Montserrat were settled four years later.

The failure of the trans-Russian route as an access to the Orient led to the development of an alternate entry through the Mediterranean and Turkey. An advantageous treaty between Elizabeth and Sultan Murad III resulted in the creation

Plate 11. Although this purports to be a picture of Columbus' landing in the Bahamas, the costumes, armor, and ships are all Elizabethan and might equally well represent a late Tudor expedition. From Theodor de Bry, *America* (1595).

of the Levant Company in 1581, and soon thereafter English trading stations began to spring up in the cities of the Ottoman dominions. Of these outposts Aleppo was by far the most important geographically, since it was the gateway to the Middle East from the Levant, whence many travelers made their way down the Euphrates valley to the Persian Gulf and beyond. Foremost of these wanderers was the adventurous Elizabethan John Newbery, who in 1581–1582 went from Aleppo to Basra, thence by ship to Ormuz in the Persian Gulf, and finally back across Persia through Isfahan and Tabriz. This journey inspired him to embark on an even more extensive venture for India and the farther Orient, and in 1583 he set out for Aleppo with five companions (of whom the chief was Ralph Fitch), sailing appropriately enough in the good ship "Tiger." From Aleppo the route of the English party took it to Baghdad and Ormuz. Here they were arrested by the Portuguese and shipped to Goa, being thus the first group of Britons ever to set foot on the Indian mainland. From their incarceration at Goa they escaped to the court of the Great Mogul Akbar at Agra and there Newbery presented an official letter to Akbar from Queen Elizabeth. Newbery then set off overland for England with the Mogul's friendly reply, only to perish mysteriously on the way. Several of the remaining English stayed behind in India, but Fitch went across country to the Ganges Delta, made his way thence to Burma and its fabled capital Pegu, and eventually reached Malacca, his farthest point, where he learned all he could about the trade to the Spice Islands and China. On his return voyage he stopped in Ceylon, then went on to Goa in disguise, and reached home via Basra and Aleppo after an absence of eight years. Fitch's trip was undoubtedly the greatest journey ever taken by an individual Englishman up to that time, and the knowledge he gained therefrom had its influence on England's eastern planning.

Fitch's journey had shown that India could be gained through the Levant, but it was equally evident that the Aleppo-Basra line was a dangerous one and only suitable for small parties. Britons had sought the Indies by the northern passages —Northwest and Northeast—and by the Strait of Magellan, to find that the last of these was thoroughly impracticable and the northern routes utterly impossible. Only the Cape route remained, which the Portuguese had been using with clockwork regularity for almost a century. Yet Portugal since 1580 had been a part of Spain, with whom England was at war, so that no diplomatic barriers prevented the subjects of Elizabeth from challenging this century-old monopoly. The publication in 1589 of the first edition of Hakluyt's *Voyages* supplied forceful propaganda for eastern trade, while assistance from the moneyed interests in the City was soon forthcoming to organize and send forth a fleet to the East Indies.

So it fell out that England's first voyage to the Orient by way of the Cape of Good Hope sailed in 1591 under the command of two distinguished veterans of the Armada fight: George Raymond and James Lancaster. Little cargo was carried, since the expedition was chiefly an exploratory one; Englishmen wanted to see whether the voyage could be made. As matters fell out, the voyage was accomplished, though only by a hair's breadth; but the Elizabethans were nothing if not persevering and they continued despite initial setbacks. The undertaking started well enough, for the Cape was reached in excellent time, but Raymond's ship went down with all hands in a typhoon off Mozambique, and Lancaster's vessel barely reached Zanzibar for much-needed repairs. When these were effected, Lancaster steered across the Indian Ocean, touched at Ceylon and Sumatra, and then proceeded to cruise in the Strait of Malacca, plundering every craft, native and Portuguese, that came his way. Fear of retaliation soon caused Lancaster to set his course for home; his crew by this time was scurvy-ridden and mutinous, and his passage around the Cape must have been perilous in the extreme. In vain he tried to gain the shelter of Bermuda, but his ship was driven back to Puerto Rico, where the mutinous crew put off their captain in the longboat and then cut the cables and sailed away—only to be

Plate 12. The famous coast pilot, translated from the original Dutch in the Armada year, with maps of the shore line from Scandinavia to Morocco. Its author, Luke Wagenaer, has enriched our language with the word "wagoner" (a volume of coastal charts).

The Mariner's Mirror is a book of great pictorial appeal.

shipwrecked soon after. Eventually Lancaster and twelve loyal sailors were picked up by a Dieppe ship and brought back to England, the sole survivors of the first English voyage to the Indies by the Cape of Good Hope.

During the closing decade of the century the Spanish War kept English ships and men fully occupied and so prevented the eastward expansion of trade. In 1592 the capture off the Azores of the great carrack "Madre de Dios" served as a reminder of the urgency of this expansion, for she carried an incredibly rich and varied cargo of Oriental commodities. During the remainder of the decade only one further attempt to reach the Indies was made—an attempt which proved even more disastrous than Lancaster's voyage. This was the expedition of Benjamin Wood, a captain who had sailed with Raleigh and Cumberland and who therefore had in him something of the pirate. Wood left England with three ships in 1596 and, having passed the Cape, touched the Indian mainland on the Malabar Coast below Goa, being thus the first English skipper ever to attain the shores of Hindustan. From Malabar, Wood made for the Strait of Malacca, plundering as he went, until in a week-long running fight with the Portuguese one of the English vessels was burnt. The remaining ship was later wrecked. Seven survivors reached Mauritius in a canoe and one man lived to be taken home to England in 1601.

These misfortunes that befell the ventures of Lancaster and Wood were all the more to be regretted since they not only set back English trade with southern Asia but also gave to England's rivals a clear field in the East Indies. In 1595–1596 a Dutch fleet had successfully made the voyage to Java, to be followed thereafter by several expeditions a year; so that when the English finally succeeded in reaching Indonesia, they found their trade rivals from Holland firmly entrenched in what was regarded as the most profitable commercial area in the entire Orient. It is all the more ironic that the principal pilot of the early Dutch voyages was John Davis of Dartmouth, the hero of the Arctic ventures of the 1580's.

Holland's success, coupled with the slackened tempo of the Spanish War, prompted the commercial interests in London to plan a more systematic policy for developing eastern trade, and sometime late in 1599 Sir Thomas Smythe and a group of influential merchants formed a joint-stock company for the purpose. This undertaking duly received its charter from the Crown on December 31, 1600—the last day of that very remarkable century—to be known eventually as the Honorable East India Company (or more simply and more colloquially as "John Company"). Such was the inception of the greatest and most famous of all the joint-stock companies; one that was to establish the British raj in India and to control its destinies until the Mutiny hardly more than a century ago.

In 1601 the Company dispatched its first voyage to the East: a fleet of four ships commanded by James Lancaster, who flew his flag in the "Red Dragon." After calling at the Cape and Madagascar and suffering much from scurvy, the squadron arrived at Achin in Sumatra, over a year after their departure from Tor Bay. So well were they received in Sumatra that one ship was loaded immediately and sent home; the others proceeded to Bantam in Java only to find that the Dutch had got there first and were securely dug in. However, a small trading post was set up and a few men were left in charge to form the first colony of Britons in the farther Orient. Lancaster then sailed for England, which he reached, after many adventures, in September, 1603. Despite a mortality of 50 per cent, he brought all his ships home with good cargoes; he had shown that the voyage could be performed, and one feels that he well deserved the knighthood that was bestowed on him.

Encouraged by this success, the Company equipped a second fleet, which sailed in March, 1604, under the command of Henry Middleton. By the end of the year the ships reached Bantam, where the factors left by Lancaster had a sorry tale to tell of relentless opposition and violence from Dutch and Javanese alike. Middleton was nevertheless able to make a good lading at this unfriendly port, and after sending some of his

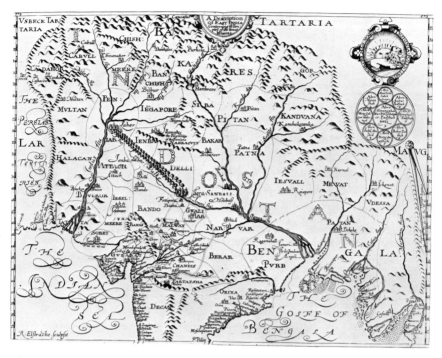

Plate 13. A map of Hindustan by William Baffin (d. 1622), a navigator equally distinguished for his exploits in the Arctic and in the Indian Ocean. Much information for this map came from Sir Thomas Roe, James I's ambassador at the court of the Great Mogul Jahangir. Note the royal road of the Moguls from Lahore to Agra; the deltas of the Ganges and the Indus; the Himalayas. Surat may be seen on the Gulf of Cambay.   From Samuel Purchas, *Hakluytus Posthumus* (1624).

fleet home he continued eastward with two ships to the Spice Islands. All along the line he met bitter hostility from the Dutch: at Banda, at Amboyna, and in the Moluccas the story was the same, and everywhere the English had the disadvantage of being the latecomers. Nevertheless, an English fleet had penetrated to the uttermost part of the East and had reached the island of Ternate in the Moluccas, where Drake had made a treaty with the Sultan a quarter-century earlier. Middleton gained England in May, 1606, with a good cargo but with heavy losses of men. The venture was regarded as a success, and Middleton, like Lancaster, received the accolade of knighthood.

Yet despite the profits of the expedition, the unrelenting shadow of Dutch monopoly must have seemed sinister to the Company, and it is not surprising that the directors accordingly dispatched the third voyage to an area untouched by the Hollanders, the Indian mainland. This expedition sailed in 1607, commanded by William Keeling, and is of special interest on account of the amateur theatricals of the crew arranged by the captain. Performances of *Hamlet* and *Richard II* were given on the deck of the "Red Dragon" while she was anchored at Sierra Leone. While Keeling himself sailed on to Bantam, his second ship, the "Hector," proceeded to Surat in the Gulf of Cambay, the deep-water port nearest to the Mogul's dominions and well to the north of the Portuguese metropolis of Goa. At this town, destined to be the Company's headquarters in India until the acquisition of Bombay in 1668, an agent was landed who went overland to Agra and was well received by Akbar's son and successor, the Emperor Jahangir. This man was William Hawkins, of the famous Tudor brood of seamen, and it may be said that his mission laid the foundation of British power in India, even though he was unable to obtain any definite trading privileges.

The success of this venture directed the Company's policy more clearly than ever toward the Asiatic mainland, although posts were still maintained in the East Indies, even in the teeth of Dutch hostility. Arabia was touched at on the fourth voyage (1609), and Siam was reached in 1612. In the following year Captain Saris reached Japan, where he was greeted at Hirado by one William Adams, who had crossed the Pacific in a Dutch ship many years previously and had since risen to a position of high esteem in Japan. But the English had to fight for every inch, not only against the Dutch and the natives, but also against the Portuguese, who warmly resented their intrusion at Surat. In two stubbornly contested naval actions in the Gulf of Cambay (Captain Best's battle in 1612 and Captain Downton's in 1615), the Britons were decisively victorious. The capture of the island stronghold of Ormuz by an Anglo-Persian armament under William Baffin (of Baffin Bay) and John Weddell in 1622 destroyed one of the key points on which the whole fabric of Portuguese power rested.

It was against this background of English victories over the Portuguese that Sir Thomas Roe made his celebrated embassage to the court of Jahangir at Agra in 1615–1618. As King James's accredited ambassador this courtly diplomat was cordially received by the Great Mogul and, after various negotiations, entered into a treaty with that monarch which eventually opened up western India to British enterprise. This was all the more fortunate because affairs in the English outposts of the Spice Islands had been going from bad to worse. Under the ruthless direction of Jan Pieterszoon Coen the Dutch company had built up a tight monopoly and would brook no intrusion from outside interests. This policy reached its peak in 1623, when the English factors and merchants throughout the Archipelago were rounded up on the Island of Amboyna by the Dutch, tortured, and slaughtered to a man. The savage "Massacre of Amboyna" caused a wave of horror throughout England, but it produced the calculated effect: the English Company relinquished all interest in the Spice Islands and devoted its efforts to the Asiatic mainland and Japan. Fortunately, by this time the Company was firmly entrenched at Surat and maintained subsidiary factories in Persia, on the Coromandel

41

Plate 14. The full-scale reconstruction of the "Susan Constant," lead ship of the three which came to Virginia in 1607, bearing the first permanent English settlers, sails in Hampton Roads. The 100-ton vessel conforms to all known specifications of the original ship and flies the Cross of St. George, flag of England in 1607, and the Union Jack, representing the then new union of England and Scotland. The vessel is on permanent exhibit at Jamestown Festival Park, Jamestown, Virginia. Photograph courtesy of the Jamestown Foundation of the Commonwealth of Virginia.

Coast, and in Japan. The foundations of the British raj had been firmly established.

The failure of Raleigh's Roanoke colony, coupled with the continuation of the Spanish War, put the progress of English settlement in North America back half a generation. With the treaty of peace in 1604, however, and with fluid capital available in the City of London, the urge for what Hakluyt called "Western Planting" became renewed. Within two years the London Company was formed, with the right to settle between the 34th and 38th parallels (between Cape Fear and Chincoteague). Its first head was Sir Thomas Smythe, who was at the same time governor of the East India Company; it also included Sir Edwin Sandys, son of the Archbishop of York, and the Earl of Southampton, Shakespeare's patron. These enthusiasts organized a party of colonists and got together a fleet which sailed in February, 1607, under the command of Captain Christopher Newport. Captain John Smith was of the company—not the premier in rank by any means, though much the most celebrated in subsequent reputation. With the flagship "Susan Constant" in the van, the little squadron took the southern track across the Atlantic from the Canaries to the Virgins and thence north to Virginia, which it reached on April 26. The colonists made a settlement on Jamestown Island shortly after, and the Virginia colony became an established fact, albeit its early days were to be extremely precarious.

In the first summer after landing John Smith and others did much valuable work in exploring the Chesapeake area, even penetrating the lower reaches of the Susquehanna on the north and attaining the present North Carolina border on the south (where, however, no trace of Raleigh's colonists was found), while the larger Virginia rivers were ascended to the fall line. But the economy of the colony was in a distressing state until John Rolfe (who married Pocahontas) conceived the idea about 1612 that the one crop that would make money in Virginia was tobacco. Meanwhile successive shipments of colonists had been cruelly decimated by malaria and deficiency diseases, and more than once the whole project was almost abandoned. The easing of the Indian menace after the colonists' retaliation for the terrible massacre of 1622 marked the turning point. After that the redskins had little more than a nuisance value; more settlers poured over from England; and the wonderfully profitable cash crop of the fragrant weed got the Old Dominion on her feet.

Meantime, one additional settlement resulted from the Virginia colony, for in 1609 the Jamestown-bound fleet of Sir George Somers was cast ashore on the rocks of Bermuda. In the course of a year several small craft were constructed from the timber of the wreckage, and the survivors were able to sail on to Virginia. This incident, however, not only inspired Shakespeare's *Tempest* but also resulted in the creation of what is today Britain's oldest colony, since the favorable report of the possibilities of Bermuda led to its permanent settlement in 1612.

Simultaneously with the creation of Virginia, exploration and colonization were being carried on in what was originally called either "Norumbega" or the "Northern Part of Virginia." A thorough reconnaissance of the Massachusetts coast was made in 1602 by Bartholomew Gosnold, who failed to winter, as he had intended, at Cuttyhunk. The next year Martin Pring, backed by Bristol interests, explored the coast of Maine, and in 1605 George Weymouth made a landfall at Nantucket and then, using Monhegan as a base, explored the St. George River and a small part of the coast nearby. Pring was back on the Maine coast in 1606, and his report on the Kennebec was so well received that a colony at its mouth was attempted by George Popham and Sir Ferdinando Gorges. The project was defeated by the severity of a down-East winter; with the coming of spring the colonists were only too glad to sail home. For some years thereafter the rock-bound coasts of Maine and Massachusetts were left alone, but in 1614 and 1615 the indefatigable John Smith made the best and most thorough exploration of the region to that date, besides bestowing on the

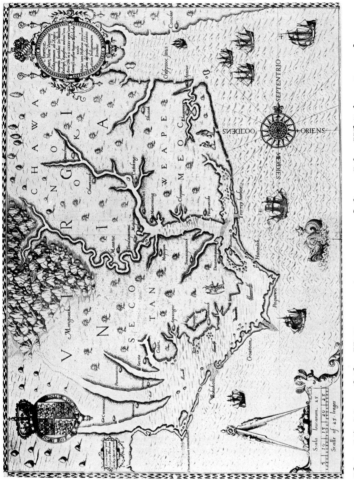

Plate 15. Map of the Hatteras region, engraved from John White's water color map, ca. 1585. From Harriot's *Brief and True Report* (1590).

45

area the name by which it has since been known—New England. His *Description of New England* (1616) with its fine map therefore had great influence on subsequent settlement, for the voyage of the "Mayflower" in 1620 and the first permanent settling in New England at Plymouth were to a large extent inspired by the pleading of this remarkable man. This, in turn, paved the way during the ensuing decade for the colonization of Massachusetts Bay, the townships of which soon surpassed Plymouth in population and prosperity.

So it was that by the beginning of the reign of Charles I the English had established permanent colonies in Virginia, Massachusetts, and the Sugar Islands of the West Indies, besides having a factory of growing importance at Surat in India, secured by a favorable treaty with the Great Mogul, as well as subsidiary posts elsewhere in India, Persia, and even Japan. Both Spain and Portugal had been vanquished at sea; the northern passages had been probed; the globe had been twice encompassed; the British Empire had been founded.

Plate 16. John Smith's map of Virginia, showing the thorough exploration of
the Chesapeake river systems made by Smith in the early years of the Jamestown colony.   From Smith's *General History of Virginia* (1624).

47

SUGGESTED READING

THE GREAT CHRONICLES

Richard Hakluyt. *The Principal Navigations, Voyages, Traffiques, and Discoveries of the English Nation.* 12 vols. Glasgow, 1903–1905.

_____. *Principall Navigations (1589).* Facsimile, ed. David B. Quinn. London, 1962.

_____. *Voyages and Documents.* Ed. Janet Hampden. (World's Classics.) Oxford, 1958.

Samuel Purchas. *Hakluytus Posthumus, or Purchas His Pilgrimes.* 20 vols. Glasgow, 1904–1907.

GENERAL WORKS

Boies Penrose. *Travel and Discovery in the Renaissance, 1420–1620.* Cambridge, Mass., 1952.

A. L. Rowse. *The Expansion of Elizabethan England.* New York, 1955.

E. G. R. Taylor. *Late Tudor and Early Stuart Geography, 1583–1650.* London, 1934.

_____. *Tudor Geography, 1485–1583.* London, 1930.

James A. Williamson. *The Ocean in English History.* Oxford, 1941.

_____. *The Tudor Age.* London, 1953.

THE EARLY PERIOD

James A. Williamson. *The Cabot Voyages and Bristol Discovery under Henry VII.* Cambridge, Eng., 1962.

_____. *Maritime Enterprises, 1485–1558.* Oxford, 1913.

_____. *The Voyages of the Cabots.* London, 1929.

VOYAGES TO SOUTH AND SOUTHWEST

Sir Julian Corbett. *Drake and the Tudor Navy.* 2 vols. London and New York, 1898.

Sir Richard Temple, ed. *The World Encompassed and Analogous Contemporary Documents concerning Sir Francis Drake's Circumnavigation of the World.* London, 1926.

Rayner Unwin. *The Defeat of John Hawkins.* New York, 1960.

Henry R. Wagner. *Sir Francis Drake's Voyage around the World.* San Francisco, 1926.

James A. Williamson. *The Age of Drake.* London, 1938.

_____. *Hawkins of Plymouth.* London, 1949.

THE NORTHERN PASSAGES

Nellis M. Crouse. *In Quest of the Western Ocean.* New York, 1928.

Edward Heawood. *A History of Geographical Discovery in the Seventeenth and Eighteenth Centuries.* Cambridge, Eng., 1912.

David B. Quinn. *The Voyages and Colonising Enterprises of Sir Humphrey Gilbert.* (Hakluyt Society.) London, 1940.

Vilhjálmur Stefansson, ed. *The Three Voyages of Martin Frobisher.* London, 1938.

THE WAR YEARS

Sir Julian Corbett. *The Successors of Drake.* London and New York, 1900.

Garrett Mattingly. *The Armada.* Boston, 1959.

Thomas Woodrooffe. *The Enterprise of England.* London, 1958.

SIR WALTER RALEIGH

David B. Quinn. *Raleigh and the British Empire.* London, 1947.

Edward J. Thompson. *Sir Walter Ralegh.* London, 1935.

Willard M. Wallace. *Sir Walter Raleigh.* Princeton, 1959.

ENGLAND IN THE EAST

Samuel C. Chew. *The Crescent and the Rose.* New York, 1937.

Sir William Foster. *England's Quest of Eastern Trade.* London, 1933.

VIRGINIA AND NEW ENGLAND

Matthew P. Andrews. *The Soul of a Nation: The Founding of Virginia and the Projection of New England.* New York, 1944.

Richard L. Morton. *Colonial Virginia.* 2 vols. Chapel Hill, 1960.

Curtis P. Nettels. *The Roots of American Civilization.* New York, 1045.

Bradford Smith, *Captain John Smith, His Life and Legend.* Philadelphia, 1953.

Louis B. Wright. *The Atlantic Frontier.* 2d ed. Ithaca, N.Y., 1959.

NAVIGATION

E. G. R. Taylor. *The Haven-finding Art.* London, 1956.

David M. Waters. *The Art of Navigation in England in Elizabethan and Early Stuart Times.* London, 1958.

CARTOGRAPHY

Gerald R. Crone. *Maps and Their Makers.* London and New York, 1953.

R. A. Skelton. *Explorers' Maps.* London, 1958.

GEOGRAPHICAL LITERATURE

Edward Lynam, ed. *Richard Hakluyt and His Successors.* London, 1946.

Franklin T. McCann. *English Discovery of America to 1585.* New York, 1952.

George B. Parks. *Richard Hakluyt and the English Voyages.* New York, 1928.